The Epic Story of the VAISAKHI SHAHEEDS

♡ | PREM RAS BOOKS

Vaisakhi Shaheeds

Copyright © 2025 Prem Ras Books, Inc.

All rights reserved.

ISBN: 9798316325818

DEDICATION

Dedicated to the thirteen Shaheeds who gave their lives on Vaisakhi 1978.

Also dedicated to Bibi Amarjit Kaur, who spent many years doing Seva for the Panth, and who recently left this world to be reunited with Bhai Fauja Singh.

TABLE OF CONTENTS

1	The Little Boy Soldier	1
2	Bad Vibes and Big Insults	8
3	Turning Into a Khalsa Boss	14
4	Marriage But Make It Khalsa	23
5	Jungle Gym	30
6	Trouble in the Air	38
7	Locked but Still Lit	45
8	The Last Langar	54
9	The Massacre	59
10	Thirteen Stories	71
11	The Aftermath	77

NOTE

All of the information in this book is based on factual research. We beg for forgiveness for any mistakes.

1 THE LITTLE BOY SOLDIER

May 17, 1936, was probably a regular hot day in Punjab. The kind where even the buffaloes look like they're too tired to blink. But in a tiny house near **Bhagupur**, something BIG happened.

A baby cried. *Loudly.*

Now, to most people, it was just another baby being born. But to this baby's dad, **Sardar Surain Singh**—a regular middle-class farmer—it was a moment straight out of a movie. I mean, they lived in a village where life was all about farming, working hard, and watching cows chew their cuds. Nothing super flashy. But still, there was something different about this kid. Like... **main character energy**.

A few days after the baby was born, the whole family walked to the village Gurdwara. You know, big white walls, sunlight bouncing off everything, super peaceful vibes. Sardar Surain Singh stood in front of Sri Guru Granth Sahib Ji while the Granthi parted open the *angs* ("pages") to take a name for the baby. It was a big moment.

And guess what name this baby got?

Vaisakhi Shaheeds

Fauja. Which means **soldier**.

Yup. Imagine being a baby and your name already sounds like you're about to win a battle. I mean, I was named after my uncle, and the only thing he ever won was a *samosa-eating contest*. From that moment, it was like the universe was setting him up for something BIG.

By the time Fauja was, like, *six or seven*, he had serious **leader energy**. The village kids totally followed him around like he was some kind of mini *general*. They'd play games in the dusty streets, and all the other boys trailed after as if he was the **king of the playground**. Races? He smoked everyone. Wrestling? He'd pin you before you could blink. Tag? Good luck—he was untouchable.

But here's the thing: it wasn't just that he was fast or strong or loud. Fauja had this vibe, like he was always thinking about the big stuff. While other kids were chasing goats or sneaking snacks, he'd be sitting there, staring off like, **Who am I? What's my purpose? What am I here for?** Yup, even at that age, he had this serious, thoughtful side.

Sometimes he'd disappear on his own and head to the **village cemetery**. Yeah - the actual place where they bury dead people. It was quiet, creepy, and full of twisty old trees. But Fauja would sit under one of them, cross-legged, eyes closed, completely still.

One night, someone spotted him there and probably thought, *Why is this kid sitting in a graveyard like it's some candy land?* So he asked him, **"Fauja, what are you doing?"**

Fauja opened his eyes, calm as ever, and said, **"I'm challenging ghosts and spirits with the Guru's Word."**

Most kids are scared of the dark. This kid was out here *confronting ghosts with Gurbani.* I mean, who *does* that?

Another time, he pulled a disappearing act. I'm not kidding. One day, this kid just took off for a WHOLE MONTH to hang out with holy men—Sants and Sadhus, the real deal. His parents were probably losing it, checking every ditch and tree in Punjab. When he strolled back home, he didn't even brag. He was just chill, like, *Yeah, I had to figure some stuff out*.

Definitely NOT your typical kid.

Then came 1947: the year of the Great *Partition*. Fauja was eleven.

India got split into two—**India** and **Pakistan**—and Punjab was caught in the chaos. People had to leave their homes, including Fauja's family. They packed up whatever they could, left Bhagupur, and moved to a place called **Gazneepur**. It was just six miles away, but everything had changed.

From the quiet fields of Bhagupur to the new start in Gazneepur, from games in dusty streets to meditating under graveyard trees, everything about Fauja Singh's childhood pointed in one direction. His name **"Fauja"** wasn't just a name. It was a hint. A promise. A mission.

It was a prophecy.

2 BAD VIBES AND BIG INSULTS

Okay, so you know how sometimes, something really bad starts with just a small whisper? Like someone says something rude in the back of class, and before you know it, the whole school's in chaos?

Well, that's kind of what happened in Punjab in the 1940s. Except it wasn't about kids fighting over lunch spots. Things were about to get *serious*.

Back when *World War II* was still going

on and people were stressed about literally everything, a new group started making noise in Punjab. They called themselves the **Nirankaris**. At first, they didn't seem like much. Just another group with opinions.

But then they started saying things like: *"**Guru Granth Sahib Ji isn't the Guru**."*

To Sikhs, this wasn't just a new idea or a different viewpoint. This was basically someone setting fire to everything sacred and then acting like it was no big deal.

At first, the Nirankaris were just a small group. But as the years rolled into the 1950s, they got louder, bolder, and more annoying by the minute. They really started making fun of Sikh beliefs, saying stuff like: *"Guru Granth Sahib? It's just a bundle of papers!"*

Which for Sikhs is basically like someone taking your heart out of your chest and trampling on it.

These guys weren't total randos. Their leader, Avtar Singh, started stirring the pot back in 1943, acting like he was some hotshot spiritual boss. Problem was, he didn't just add his own weird ideas—he flipped Sikh beliefs into a pretzel.

In Sikhi, after Guru Gobind Singh Ji, the one and only Guru forever is Sri Guru Granth Sahib Ji. It's not just a book; it's the *living Guru*, the heart of everything.

But Avtar Singh? He's like, **Nah, I'm the Guru now,** trying to start his own knockoff Guru franchise.

Now imagine you're the young teenage Fauja. You've got that fire in you, already feeling something bigger pulling at your soul. Then you hear these clowns trash-talking everything you love. We don't have a play-by-play of how he reacted back then, but come on—if someone insulted your mom and then yeeted your dog across the yard, you'd never forget it. This? Way worse.

Fast-forward to the 1970s, and they've got a new guy in charge: **Gurbachana**.

This dude's got zero chill. He brags, **"Guru Gobind Singh Ji made 5 Beloved Ones? Watch me make 7!"** Like he's in a Guru showdown. Total ego explosion.

Then he starts dropping articles like, *"All Guru Gobind Singh Ji wasn't a saint, he just swung swords,"* and—yep—insults Guru Granth Sahib Ji again, calling it a *"bulky collection."* But the absolute worst? He threatens to put his nasty foot on Sri Guru Granth Sahib Ji. Not kidding. *Actual foot.*

If you're Sikh, you get how insane that is. We don't even step near Guru Sahib without covering our heads and ditching our shoes.

And it keeps going. The Nirankaris roast big Sikh figures—*Mata Tripta Ji, Bhagat Kabir Ji, Bhai Lalo Ji*, even *Bibi Nanaki Ji*. Decades of nonstop shade.

Here's the kicker: the government leaders? They're just sitting there, twiddling their thumbs. People are fuming, but the big shots are like, "*Meh, it's whatever.*" Newsflash: it was NOT whatever.

By now, Fauja's in his thirties. He's not that wide-eyed kid anymore. That spark from way back? It's a full-on wildfire. The time's coming when he's gonna step up and yell, "Enough already!"

Someone's gotta clap back. Soon.

3 TURNING INTO A KHALSA BOSS

Que in the 1950s. Fauja was older now. Not the ghost-challenging kid anymore. He had passed his tenth class and off he went to **Khalsa College in Amritsar.**

For most students, this would've been a dream. But not for Fauja.

He liked the books and all, but something wasn't clicking. No matter how much he read, he felt like he was still missing something. Something real. Something that wasn't in a textbook.

So... *he dropped out.*

Yup, he yeeted himself out of there and ran off on a mission to go *find God*. His family freaked out, like, **Uh, where's our kid?!** They were legit putting ads in newspapers, basically the 1960s version of "HAVE YOU SEEN THIS GUY?"

Turns out, he was just chilling with some old Sadhus.

For **two whole years**, Fauja followed them. He walked dusty trails, sat in makeshift ashrams, and basically lived off spiritual vibes and devotion. And these weren't the soft, sweet holy men you see in movies. These guys were **hardcore**.

No comfort. No phone. No "snacks after 10." Just the open sky, long stretches of silence, and serious soul-searching. Fauja sat meditating with them for hours, listened to the old Sadhus, and absorbed every bit of spiritual wisdom he could. He wasn't there to mess around—he was on a mission to find God, not to snap pics for his Instagram.

One of the Sadhus even gave him a **Mantar**—a sacred chant—to help him focus. Fauja took it seriously. Like, *really seriously*. He stuck with it, hoping it would lead him to the connection he'd been chasing for years.

But here's the thing:
It didn't work.

The thing he was looking for?
This wasn't it.

Meanwhile, his family back in Gazneepur was **panicking**. They hadn't heard from him in forever. When Fauja finally realized that chilling with the Sadhus wasn't giving him what he was looking for, he finally came back home.

His family was probably thinking, ***Okay, he's done being a hippie now. Time to be normal.*** NOPE. *Not even close.*

In 1964, everything flipped. Fauja went to this massive Kirtan **Smagam** run by the "Akhand Kirtani Jatha". Think epic kirtan jams, a *huge* crowd, and Sri Guru Granth Sahib Ji front and center. That's when he realized: ***"I know what I've been looking for."***

There, in the presence of the **Guru Granth Sahib Ji**, surrounded by the sound of Gurbani, he made his decision: he was going to take Amrit and get the *real* Mantar of NAAM. This wasn't something some worldly Sadhu could give him. Only the True Guru could give it to him... *and he would give his head just to get it.*

The ceremony was powerful. The **Panj Pyare** stirred the Amrit with a Khanda,

Vaisakhi Shaheeds

reciting Gurbani as Fauja knelt before them. As the sacred nectar touched his eyes and lips, it wasn't just a ritual. As the Naam Mantar entered his soul, it was like he *died* and was *born again.*

It was a full-on **Khalsa upgrade**.

From then on, he wasn't just Fauja. He was ***Bhai Fauja Singh***. Warrior. Holy roller. Basically a Sikh superhero without the cape. He started rocking the full *Bana*: long *Chola*, *Kirpan* strapped on, the five Ks, the whole deal. He was officially in the Guru's squad now.

And he didn't stop there. Bhai Fauja Singh started training in Gatka. And guess what? *He crushed it.* Like, people would try to take him on, and he'd just twirl his stick and send them packing, all calm-like. Total legend.

But here's the kicker—he wasn't doing this to flex. He wasn't posting "#GatkaGoals" or anything. He was getting ready. For what? He didn't say. He also got into this thing called **Sarbloh Bibek**, where you only eat food cooked in iron by meditating on Naam. He was all about keeping it pure and simple—Khalsa style.

People started whispering, kinda like, "***Yo, Fauja, why you so obsessed with fighting stuff? It's chill right now. Just sing some Shabads and relax.***" But Fauja wasn't here for chill. He'd read the history books—Sikhs versus

Vaisakhi Shaheeds

Mughals, all that jazz—and he had this gut feeling. Something **big** was coming. Something *not-so-chill*.

While everyone else was like, "*Let's just vibe,*" Bhai Fauja Singh was all, "***I promised my head to my Guru. If he calls for it, I'm giving it.***" No big speech, no drama—just straight-up, quiet "I'm ready" energy.

That day in 1964? It wasn't the end of his story. It was the start of him becoming a total **Khalsa boss**. From tiny villages to massive showdowns, from quiet mornings to wild battles, Bhai Fauja Singh was locked in on the path he picked. And he wasn't turning back.

4 MARRIAGE, BUT MAKE IT KHALSA

By 1965, Bhai Fauja Singh was not your average 28-year-old. While most dudes his age were stressing over boring stuff like jobs—or, I dunno, trying not to burn roti—he'd already **taken Amrit**, joined the Khalsa, become a Gatka ninja, and basically turned into a *spiritual superhero*. Normal? Nope. Awesome? Yep.

So, what's his next move? He decides to get married.

Vaisakhi Shaheeds

The date? *April 13th, Vaisakhi.* Enter **Bibi Amarjit Kaur**, stage left.

Now, get this—before they tied the knot, Bhai Fauja Singh made two big promises:

1. He'd cook his own food. Most husbands at that time would have been like, ***"Hey stay in the kitchen, wifey!"*** But he didn't make Bibi Amarjit Kaur do it for him. That was *his* job.
2. No kids. Not because he didn't like them—he totally did—but because he saw every Gursikh kid as his own, and they'd be taking care of a lot of people.

They got married that Vaisakhi day in Amritsar. Together, they turned their marriage into a *Seva factory*. Their house was basic—no fancy couches or shiny gadgets—but the door was always open. Gursikhs crashing for the night? Travelers needing a snack? Random Sangat members? Come on in! It was like a 24/7 Khalsa Airbnb, minus the Wi-Fi.

Their place? Third floor, no running water. Sounds like a total drag, right? Except Bhai Fauja Singh turned it into a flex. Every day, he'd wake up for **Amrit Vela** (that's super early), trudge down those creaky stairs to the pump, and haul buckets of water all the way back up—*happily*, like it was some game.

Someone once was like, ***Erm, why not***

just get a water system?

He goes, *"If I did that, I'd miss out on this Seva!"*

Who even thinks like that? This soldier turned chores into a spiritual glow-up.

Bhai Fauja Singh wasn't just preaching this stuff—he lived it. One time, he told Bibi Amarjit Kaur, *"All the money we spend on ourselves is wasted, but the money we spend on Seva? That's going straight to our real bank—the one that matters."*

Deep, right? Meanwhile, most of us are over here panicking if someone asks us to borrow three bucks.

They weren't rolling in cash, but every penny they had went to the **Panth**—*Langar, Smagams,* you name it. And they didn't just sit back and write checks, either. Bhai Fauja Singh was out there teaching Gatka to kids and teens—not just the cool flips and sword moves, but the *vibe*. He mixed **Bir Ras** (that's warrior energy) with **Naam Ras** (love for Vaheguru's Name) like some kind of Sikh smoothie.

And Bibi Amarjit Kaur? Her kirtan game was unreal. Her voice could hit you right in the soul, and she'd sing at Smagams all over Punjab while Bhai Fauja Singh fired up the crowd with his fearless energy.

Total. Power. Couple.

Vaisakhi Shaheeds

So yeah, their marriage wasn't just some mushy love story. It was a full-on mission. Two Khalsay, side by side, keeping it simple, and staying laser-focused on the Panth.

And with the Nirankaris stirring up more drama and disrespect every day, this dream team was about to get real important, real fast.

5 JUNGLE GYM
(BUT FOR KHALSAY)

Okay, so it's the 70s now.

While most people were kicking back, maybe growing some wheat or arguing about who'd win in a buffalo race, Bhai Fauja Singh was staring down a 50-60 acre jungle in Gazneepur.

And I'm not talking about some messy backyard with overgrown grass. This was a legit wilderness — thorns, giant trees, and stuff that basically screamed, "Stay away, dude!"

Everyone else saw it and was like, "Hard pass."

Bhai Fauja Singh saw it and was like, *"Oh yeah, this is it."*

So here's the deal: this land came from his dad after Partition, when borders got all messy and people had to move. Most folks would've sold it or ignored it like a forgotten homework assignment. Not Bhai Fauja Singh. He looked at this jungle and saw a Khalsa playground just begging to be unleashed.

His big plan? Three steps:
1. **Clear the wild mess.**

2. Build a farm.
3. Make it a hardcore Sikh headquarters — think Gatka practice, Gurbani vibes, and total life-changing awesomeness.

Picture this: part spiritual retreat, part ninja training camp, part free food zone, and 100% Khalsa central.

He rounded up a squad of Singhs from Amritsar—Bibi Amarjit Kaur included, because she was basically his MVP—and they got to work. No fancy machines, just hands, basic tools, and a whole lot of grit. Chopping, digging, dragging—they turned that jungle into something real, step by sweaty step.

This wasn't some half-baked project

either, like when you start a fort and ditch it after two hours. Nope, this was serious business.

One day, Bhai Fauja Singh strolled into a nearby village, rocking his Kirpan out loud and proud, which wasn't exactly normal back then. He brought **Giani Hazoora Singh** along and dropped a speech that basically set the place on fire (not literally... *yet*). He wasn't farming for cash, he said. This was for the Panth—a spot where Sikhs could train, sing, and become Khalsa-level warriors.

By the end, village kids were signing up like it was a superhero tryout. **Boom**—Khalsa Farm had its first crew.

Vaisakhi Shaheeds

Fast forward to 1974, and things leveled up.

Kirtan sessions kicked off—open-air, full volume.

Bibi Amarjit Kaur led the charge with her voice, which hit like a thunderstorm.

Langar rolled out, and guess who was dishing out rotis? Bhai Fauja Singh, kneading dough like he was born for it.

The energy? Off the charts.

The villagers were shook. Amritdhari Sikhs weren't super common around there, but now they were popping up everywhere—serving food, belting out

Gurbani, rocking full Bana, and owning it. Even the ladies started tying *Dastaars* after watching Bibi Amarjit Kaur do her thing. Total game-changer.

But, because life loves a plot twist, stuff went sideways.

One day in 1974, right before the first harvest, chaos hit.

FIRE.

Bibi Joginder Kaur—an older lady who treated Bhai Fauja Singh like her own kid—was there, cooking Langar in the outdoor kitchen. Then, out of nowhere, a crazy wind swooped in, and BAM—flames everywhere. The kitchen setup, some huts, tools, supplies—all torched. Everyone freaked. Well, almost everyone.

Bhai Fauja Singh strolled out of the fields, saw the smoke, and... laughed. **Laughed!** Then he grinned at Bibi Joginder Kaur and was basically like, ***Chill, this is the Guru's plan.***

Like, who even reacts like that?!

That was him, though—cool as ice when everything's burning down. For him, it wasn't about the stuff getting wrecked. It was about the mission.

And that mission? Still kicking.

Khalsa Farm wasn't just dirt and

crops. It was a vibe—a loud-and-proud "The Khalsa's here, deal with it" kind of statement.

They had no clue the real storm was coming—one that'd rattle all of Punjab. But for now, Khalsa Farm stood tough, stubborn, and packed with people ready to go all-in for the Guru.

.

6 TROUBLE IN THE AIR

Okay, so by this time Bhai Fauja Singh was living like every day was straight out of a superhero movie. *Mission mode:* ON.

And trust me, there was a mission. A BIG one.

The Nirankaris were still around, and their leader, Gurbachana, had gone full-on supervillain. He wasn't just annoying anymore—he was basically running an *anti-Sikhi* tour across Punjab.

Anyway, Bhai Fauja Singh? He was NOT here for it. By now he's in his mid-30s, and his life's basically a checklist of epic stuff: serving the Sangat, reciting Gurbani, teaching Gatka, and doing Seva like it's his full-time job. But this Nirankari nonsense? It hit him right in the feels. Like, not just *"ugh, that's annoying"* feels. More like *"someone's trash-talking my whole family and I'm about to throw down"* feels.

So, in 1972, something wild happens.

There's this spot called **Misri Bazar**, right? And some loser decides to disrespect Guru Granth Sahib Ji in the WORST way. They went there ready to tear up Guru Sahib's **Saroop**. You'd think the cops would swoop in like, "**Not today, buddy!**" But nope. They're just standing there, twiddling their thumbs like they're waiting for a memo from the boss.

Guess who doesn't wait for memos? Bhai Fauja Singh.

He's out there inspecting farms by day, but when he hears about this, he's like, "**It's going down.**" History doesn't spill all the tea on what he did, but let's just say he rolled up, handled it, and those punks turned tail REAL quick. Problem solved, right?

WRONG. Get this: a bunch of Sikhs were like, *"Shhh, don't tell anyone! It might start a fight between Hindus and Sikhs!"* And this had Bhai Fauja Singh going, **"What's *happened* to the Khalsa Panth?"**

That question stuck in his brain like gum on a shoe.

Then, 1975 hits, and it's déjà vu all over again. October 17—a chill day of prayers and Langar at **Gurdwara Bhai Salo Ji**—gets totally wrecked. Some goons show up, trash the place, beat up the Granthi, ***disrespect Guru Sahib***, and then—because apparently that wasn't enough—they're like, **"Oh, and we're burning down another Gurdwara tonight. See ya!"**

Okay, that's it. Lines have been CROSSED.

Bhai Fauja Singh hears about this and doesn't even blink. He grabs a few Singhs, and they're off like the Khalsa Avengers. First stop: Gurdwara Bhai Salo Ji to check the damage. Next stop: **Gurdwara Guru Keh Mehal**, where these losers are planning their big bonfire. Except now the goons are playing hide-and-seek in tall buildings, chucking bricks, stones, and—get this—acid bottles. ACID. Who even has that lying around?

But Fauja Singh and his crew? They're not fazed. They're out there in full "Khalsa mode," holding the line like bosses. No running. No quitting. Moving like lightening. *Every move precise.*

The attackers try to hold their ground, but they're no match. With cries of **"Bolay So Nihaal, Sat Sri Akaal!"** echoing through the air, the defenders push them back.

Then, in the middle of the fight, someone lands a heavy blow right on Bhai Fauja Singh. He staggers, blood soaking through his kurta—but he doesn't stop. Not until the last attacker is gone.

They come out looking like they just survived a war movie—blood, ripped clothes, the works—but the Gurdwara? *Saved.*

And the police? Crickets. Not a peep. No "Hey, great job, guys!" No "Let's stop this madness!" Just... nothing.

At this point, Bhai Fauja Singh's not confused anymore. He gets it. He turns to Bibi Amarjit Kaur one day and drops this total mic-drop line: **"Guru Gobind Singh Ji made the Khalsa with his blood. When the Khalsa plant starts drying up, it needs more blood to grow. That's when the Guru's beloved ones step up and spill theirs to keep it alive."**

While everyone else is pretending nothing's wrong, Bhai Fauja Singh's mentally preparing. Because his big debut is coming fast. And he's ready.

7 LOCKED BUT STILL LIT

Okay, if you thought Bhai Fauja Singh was a total legend before, buckle up, because 1977 was when he turned the intensity up to eleven.

He was 41, basically the superhero of Punjab by now—everybody knew him as the guy who'd take on anyone messing with the innocent or disrespecting Sikhi. But that year? Oh man, things got wild. Like, "jail time" wild.

Here's the scoop on what went down:

First up, there was this innocent Hindu woman—nobody wrote down her name—who got seriously messed up by the police. And I'm not talking about a stern lecture. I mean *horror movie* bad. Her husband was running around, begging judges and religious bigwigs for help, but they all just shrugged. Then someone whispered, **"*There's this Singh in Amritsar who doesn't play around.*"**

Boom. Bhai Fauja Singh enters the chat.

He heard the story, rounded up a couple of his toughest Singhs, and marched right into that police station like it was a video game boss level. What they found was awful. The woman was still there, completely broken by what had happened. The officers who had done it? *Still walking around like nothing was wrong.*

Bhai Fauja Singh swooped in and got her out of there faster than you can say "justice." But wait—**plot twist**—he didn't stop there. He made sure those crooked cops got a taste of their own medicine. How? Nobody's spilling the tea on that one, but it was big enough to **land him in jail**.

Did he care? Nope. Not even a little.

After he got out of jail the first time, came round two.

Some dude was harassing (or should I say *torturing*) a Singhni—like, nonstop. Bhai Fauja Singh rolled up, all calm and polite, and said, **"You better stop. I'm warning you."** The guy didn't listen.

Things got heated. The guy pulled a weapon, thinking he was tough. Bhai Fauja Singh gave him one last warning, like, **This is your final shot, dude**. The guy laughed in Bhai Fauja Singh's face.

Worst. Move. EVER.

I won't get into details, but let's just say this: it was **game over** for this guy... *forever.* Bhai Fauja Singh made it VERY clear that harassing women wasn't going to be tolerated in *any* corner of the village.

Justice: 1. Jerk: 0.
Khalsa-style.

Then there was incident number three, and this one was brutal.

Some punk assaulted a Sikh woman, ***damaging her for life***. The entire community was in shock, heartbroken. Bhai Fauja Singh tried talking sense into him first, like, **"Don't you know that we should treat our sisters and daughters like they're sacred?"** The guy smirked and said, **"I'll do it again, and nobody's stopping me."**

Big mistake. Bhai Fauja Singh looked him dead in the eye and was like, ***Oh-yeah, hotshot?*** BOOM... And that was it—*donezo*. That guy would never have the chance to hurt another girl, EVER AGAIN.

Bhai Fauja Singh was putting everything on the line to protect his community from these goons. Bibi Amarjit Kaur was even like, **"One case isn't even wrapped up, and you're already in another mess?"** Yeah, it was *that* kind of year.

All this craziness landed Bhai Fauja Singh in jail. Most people would've freaked out or cried about it, but not him. Oh no. He was straight-up glowing in there.

He set up his own little kitchen to cook his food, turned his cell into a mini

Vaisakhi Shaheeds

Gurdwara, and even started writing poetry. He only wrote one poem, called **"Kurbani,"** but holy cow, it's intense. Here's how it went:

For your Sikhi, O Guru so true,
With thought, word, and deed, we'll honor you.
Our wealth, our youth, all that we own,
To the Panth's cause, our lives we've sown.

This body, kept since childhood's morn,
Will serve your call when need is born.
Your Bani dwells within our soul,
Cleansing flaws to make us whole.

With Grace, O Lord, so kind, so near,
Limb by limb, we'll persevere.
Your Name's a treasure, flag so grand,
We'll wave it high o'er every land.

The fading light we see decline,
With our blood, we'll make it shine.
Mind's wisdom cast, O Giver great,
Our light with yours will blend, our fate.

Vaisakhi Shaheeds

Your timeless faith, so pure, so strong,
Defies all evil, rights the wrong.
Faith's symbols dim, now tucked away,
Through sacrifice, we'll bring their day.

By your Grace, the Khalsa cries,
Our inner voice shall pierce the skies.
Sikhi's nectar, deathless stream,
With hair and breath, we'll live its dream.

When life's last hour comes to call,
Our heads we'll give—*we'll sacrifice all*.

That's not just poetry. That's a hype song for a revolution.

The jail staff? Totally shook. Inmates started taking Amrit left and right. Even the warden's son was like, ***"Sign me up for the Khalsa crew!"*** They let the Jatha throw a full-on Rainsbhai (*all-night*) Kirtan inside the jail—

imagine that, a holy jam session behind bars.

By the end of 1977, he was out on bail, back to doing Seva and spreading the word like nothing happened. But here's the thing—there was this weird vibe in the air. Like when you know a storm's about to hit, but the sky's still quiet. He'd faced down injustice three times, ended up in jail, and didn't even flinch. Something tells me he knew, deep down, that the next big fight was coming—and it was gonna be the wildest one yet.

8 THE LAST LANGAR

By early 1978, there was this super weird vibe in Punjab. You know that feeling when everything looks totally normal—like, kids playing, birds chirping—but your gut's screaming, "Uh-oh, something HUGE is coming"?

Yeah, that's what it was like.

The Nirankaris were getting way too bold, acting like they owned the place.

The Panth? Totally fed up and hurting. And Bhai Fauja Singh? He was just strolling around at 41 years old, calm as ever, like he had a secret memo that said, GET READY, DUDE.

He had already done it all—stood up to jerks, got thrown in jail for justice, built a farm from nothing, and taught kids Gatka like a pro. But in early 1978, something flipped.

He started dropping these heavy lines to Bibi Amarjit Kaur, like: **"Picture my dead body in your head. Can you handle it? Stay tough and don't despair."**

Then came April 11—two days before Vaisakhi (which was also their wedding anniversary). He rolled up to her school where she was a teacher to walk her home, like he always did. But this time, with all her teacher buddies standing there, he just laid it out: **"The divine call's coming."**

Weird thing to say, right?

And then—April 12, the day before Vaisakhi. There was a Smagam going down near Sri Darbar Sahib, and Bhai Fauja Singh was there, barefoot, keeping it simple, zero distractions, doing Langar Seva.

Some other high-flying Singhs had arrived there, too. **Bhai Avtar Singh**, a farmer, who'd told his family, "Stick to Sikhi no matter what," right before leaving. **Bhai Raghbir Singh**, ex-soldier turned compositor, who hauled himself over from Sunam just to vibe with the Sangat. And **Bhai Gurcharan Singh**, who straight-up ditched his first college exam to show up (my parents would have killed me if I ever pulled that). And a whole bunch of other gangster Gurmukhs. Basically, the place was *packed* with literal spiritual superheroes.

That night, the Smagam kept rolling under the stars—Kirtan, Naam, Sangat, the whole deal buzzing like the air was electric. And Bhai Fauja Singh? He just sat there, soaking it all in. Quiet. Steady. Ready.

By the time the sun popped up the next

morning, everything would flip upside down. Vaisakhi was about to bring a moment that'd shake the Panth to its core.

And Bhai Fauja Singh, chill as ever, wasn't just ready—he'd been waiting for this moment his whole life.

9 THE MASSACRE

Vaisakhi morning, April 13, 1978, in Amritsar, began with Kirtan. It felt like stepping back to 1699, when Guru Gobind Singh Ji created the Khalsa. Total throwback vibes.

Since Amrit Vela, the place was alive. The Langar hall was jammed with people, kirtan echoed everywhere, and Bhai Fauja Singh? He was right in the middle of it, sleeves rolled up, hands buried in flour, kneading dough like he was on a mission.

But then, around 10 a.m., everything flipped.

Suddenly, the loudspeaker crackled to life, and an announcement pierced the air: "Nirankaris are marching through the streets and yelling insults at Sri Guru Granth Sahib Ji."

Bam. Everyone stopped dead.

Bhai Fauja Singh stood up—calm, quiet, intense. He brushed the flour off his hands, stepped out to where Sangat was gathering in hushed murmurs. Standing tall, his booming voice urged the Sangat that they could not tolerate these attacks on their beloved

Guru any more.

Then he crouched down and made a line in the dirt. **"Sikho,"** he said, **"if you're ready to give your heads to your Guru today, cross this line."**

You could hear the air get heavy. It was like it was Vaisakhi 1699, all over again.

Then—*step, step, step*. One by one, people began to cross over: men, women, and even children. 100 people, 200 people - maybe even 300 people. *All ready to stand up for their Guru.*

An Ardas was done. Everyone bowed low before Guru Granth Sahib Ji—foreheads to the floor—then stood tall. No yelling, no chaos. Just Gurbani

humming from their lips.
They started walking.

First stop: **Ramdas Niwas**, where the Nirankaris had passed. But the procession was already done. So they turned toward the real problem—the Nirankari gathering near **Rigo Bridge**. The loudspeakers was still blasting there, insults flying over the crowds like a slap in the face.

But before they could get close—BAM, police everywhere. A human wall.

The Gursikhs explained: *it's just a peaceful protest, no weapons.* One officer nodded.

"Hold up here. I'll talk to them."

So they waited. *Thirty long minutes.*

And the whole time? The Nirankaris kept trash-talking. Loud. Nonstop. Nobody shutting them down.

The officer came back with more cops, including the Superintendent of Police, a guy named **DSP Joshi**. **"It's done already,"** he said gruffly. ***"Go home."***

Except it wasn't done. The loudspeakers were still going. Everyone could hear it.

And then...
Everything exploded.

Out of nowhere, the Nirankari crowd— ***five or six thousand strong***—came

charging like a tsunami. These weren't just random angry dudes. They were in uniforms, organized, and loaded with weapons like *they'd been planning this.*

And I mean **loaded.** Some fired rifles and pistols, bullets zipping through the air. Others swung swords, spears, and axes, while arrows flew overhead. A few even tossed acid bottles and homemade bombs—BOOM, fire and smoke everywhere.

The Gursikhs? No guns. No shields. Some didn't even have *shoes*—just their Bana, their Kirpans, and their guts. And they didn't bolt.

They held their ground.

Bullets hit first. CRACK, CRACK, CRACK—Singhs started dropping. But it didn't stop there. If someone fell, the attackers started hacking them with axes, swords, bricks, *anything* they could swing. **Brutal** doesn't even *cover it*.

And right up front? Bhai Fauja Singh.

He didn't back off. Didn't even flinch. Just kept moving. Then—WHAM—something (maybe a bullet, maybe a spear) smashed into his eye. Blood gushed down his face, soaking his white chola red.

But he didn't budge. He yanked open the end of his **dumala**, and wrapped it tight around his head to stop the bleeding, and kept going. But here's the kicker—word from the old-timers says when the attack hit, Bhai Fauja Singh didn't just stand there. He fought back, swinging his Kirpan like a champ, taking on anyone who got close. Half-blind, blood everywhere, and he's still charging like a lion.

"SINGHO!" he shouted, voice cutting through the chaos. **"Push forward! Now's the time to die fighting!"**

Even half-broken, with smoke choking the air and bullets whizzing by, he was still the leader. His voice didn't crack. It *roared*.

Vaisakhi Shaheeds

Around him, the Singhs kept chanting Gurbani and Naam. Some were bleeding, turbans dangling, but they kept moving. No screams. No panic. The worse it got, the braver they looked. Then the police turned it up a notch—*in the worst way.*

Instead of stopping the Nirankaris, they jumped in—on the *wrong* side. Tear gas canisters flew, landing right in the Gursikhs' faces. Some officers even started shooting at them, picking their team loud and clear.

And then the worst part hit.

DSP Joshi marched up to Bhai Fauja Singh, pulled out his .32-caliber pistol, and unloaded it—six bullets, BAM-

BAM-BAM—right into his chest.

But Bhai Fauja Singh didn't collapse.

He just stood there, breathing hard, blood everywhere, gasping, "Vaheguru... Vaheguru... Vaheguru...."

Two Singhs ran over, saw he was still alive, and tried to drag him to safety. But they didn't get far—as soon as the police saw this, they literally nabbed them and hauled them off.

Then they grabbed Bhai Fauja Singh— still breathing—and threw him into a "dead wagon," some beat-up truck for hauling dead bodies.

That's it, just like that. As if he was a

sack of nothingness. As if _he_ was the bad guy.

Another Singh found him a few minutes, lying there, still muttering "Vaheguru." Alive, barely.

That loser, DSP Joshi? Well, he made sure that no doctor got near him. It wasn't just death. It was a shutdown.

And by the time Bibi Amarjit Kaur had managed to fight her over way to him, it was over. His last breath was gone. He had passed on, chanting Naam 'till his last.

10 THIRTEEN STORIES

So, the smoke finally started clearing, and the streets got all quiet. But it wasn't because the chaos was done—it was because **thirteen** Singhs had just become Shaheed, and over seventy others were sprawled out, bleeding like something from a war movie.

Thirteen. Sounds like a small number, right? Like, big deal, it's not a hundred. But each of those Singhs? They were basically walking legends. Every one of them had a story that could fill its own book.

Take **Bhai Avtar Singh** from Kurala, Hoshiarpur. Born in 1912, so he was, like, 66—old enough to be your grandpa. But you'd never guess it. He took Amrit in 1961 and went full Sarbloh Bibek mode—eating only from iron pots cooked by Amritdhari hands. Total hardcore. His whole life was this disciplined, no-nonsense vibe.

When the attack hit, a bullet slammed into him. He dropped. But instead of flopping over like a normal person, he *sat up*—legs crossed, chill as anything—and started chanting Naam. **Loud**. Like, louder than the gunshots, people said. Even when the Nirankaris came swinging lathis and *bashed his head in*, he didn't flinch. Just kept chanting Naam, until he was gone.

I don't know how else to say it—**he left like a saint.**

Then there's **Bhai Raghbir Singh** from Bhagupur, Amritsar. Only 29. He loved to do Kirtan, and man, could he sing. His vibes were so good, it'd hit you right in the feels.

He was shot in the chest. Hit with lathis. His bones were *broken*. But the whole time, he was still reciting the Guru's Naam. And when he left this world, it was while singing the same praises he had spent his whole life singing.

Bhai Gurcharan Singh from Rurka Korad, Jullundur, was 32. Total lover of seva—always at it. He'd memorized a lot of Gurbani from a young age, and it showed. They say he fell mid-chant, his voice slicing through the screams and sirens. Body hit the ground, but his spirit? **Untouchable.**

There were more, too. **Bhai Harbhajan Singh** from Bhattian. **Bhai Piara Singh** from Bhungrani. **Bhai Gurdial Singh** from Mode. Bullets, blades, whatever—they got hit with it all. But they never stopped japping Naam. People couldn't get over how their lips kept moving, even as they dropped.

Then you've got **Bhai Amrik Singh** from Khujala, **Bhai Dharambir Singh** from

Ajeet Nagar, and **Bhai Kewal Singh** from Prem Garh. Cornered, beaten, hacked up—they could've bolted. Nope. They took it like their spirits were made of iron, not their swords.

Bhai Hari Singh, Bhai Ranbir Singh Fauji, and **Baba Darshan Singh**? Same deal. Bullets ripping through them. Swords slashing. Blood everywhere. And still, they're breathing Naam as they peace out.

You could call it just bravery, sure. But it was bigger than that. Like, you'd feel it in your gut even if you were miles away. A buzz. A jolt. Something *powerful*. Something... that would be remembered forever.

Vaisakhi Shaheeds

11 THE AFTERMATH
(AKA the day everything would change)

April 15, 1978: NOT your average day. Nope. Not even in the same universe.

Just two days after the massacre, Amritsar was weirdly sombre. Like, almost as if even the pigeons were holding their breath. But it wasn't a *scared* kind of quiet.

More like, *something's-coming*-quiet.

By the time the sun peeked out, Gurdwara Ramsar Sahib was stuffed with 25,000 to 30,000 Sikhs—shoulder to shoulder. And here's the wild part: people weren't bawling their eyes out. No tissues. No pity party.

They showed up to honour.

The thirteen Shaheed Singhs—Bhai Fauja Singh and the rest of the crew—were lined up on this ginormous funeral pyre. The police had tried stashing their bodies in the morgue like some creepy evidence locker, but the Sangat was like, "Nah, we're doing this our way." Even in death, these guys were a squad.

When they lit that fire? Oh man, it wasn't just flames. It was a full-on statement. A Khalsa-sized roar.

The smoke shot up like a boss, screaming to the world: **These Singhs didn't flop. They stood tall—bullets, swords, whatever—and now they're chilling with Vaheguru.**

Bibi Amarjit Kaur was right there in the crowd. You know her—the lady who was Bhai Fauja Singh's MVP and should have been celebrating her wedding anniversary with him.

Now she's at his cremation, and guess what? No sobbing. No fainting. Just pure, unbreakable calm.

Bhai Fauja Singh had laid it out for her: **"Don't cry when you see my body. Stay strong."**

And she did. She stood there like a brick wall—like her soul was forged in the same fire now blasting into the sky.

The whole thing hit like a thunderclap. You could feel it rattling your ribs.

Sant Jarnail Singh Bhindranwale stood there among the crowd, grim-faced. He'd been in Amritsar when the massacre went down, and now he was here, and you could see the fire in his eyes. As he looked at the bodies of his brothers, you could see a storm brewing beneath the surface of his skin.

Punjab had been a mess for years – run over by evil and corrupt people. They'd been terrorizing Sikhs for far too long. And now this was the straw that broke the camel's back.

You could feel it in the entire crowd. Fists tightened. Eyes narrowed.

There was still a line in the sand. And a whole lot of Khalsa was about to cross over.

AFTERNOTE

So, the Vaisakhi Massacre was done. Thirteen Singhs—martyred. Blood still fresh on the ground from April 13, 1978. You'd think everyone would just go home and sulk, right? Wrong. This wasn't the end. This was the beginning of something huge.

See, Sikhs were mad. Not just "I lost my favorite toy" mad. This was deep, boiling, "we're not taking this anymore" mad. For years—decades, even—they'd been dealing with disrespect. The Nirankaris had been at it since the 1940s, trashing Guru Granth Sahib Ji, twisting Gurbani, acting like Sikh beliefs were a joke. And the government? They'd just shrug—like, "Eh, whatever." Often they'd even back the jerks, like when the police shot at unarmed Singhs during the massacre. That day in Amritsar? It was the tipping point.

Punjab was a mess back then. Cops hurting innocent people, leaders backing criminals, Nirankaris strutting around and turning everyone against the Sikhs. Sikhs had been patient—*super* patient—but after seeing thirteen of their own cut down, they were done. Done with the insults. Done with the unfairness. Done with all the shady stuff piling up. This wasn't just about one fight. It was about saying, "No more."

After that day, Sikhs didn't just sit quiet. The massacre flipped a switch. They started pushing back—hard. Sant Jarnail Singh emerged from the dust of the massacre, started getting louder, rallying people against the mess in Punjab. It wasn't about revenge—it was about justice. And that fight? It was coming. You could feel it brewing, like a storm nobody could stop.

Because when thirteen Singhs give their lives, and 30,000 show up to say goodbye, that's not a defeat. That's a promise. A promise that the Khalsa doesn't bend—it rises. And rise it would.

Yo... bruh! What did you think of the book?

If you liked it, check out more lit books from:

www.PremRas.org

(Or else. I'll use more Gen Z slang on you... don't make me do it, aii?)

Made in the USA
Las Vegas, NV
09 April 2025